Table of Contents

Picket Fence Holder & Butterfly

Skill Level

 **INTERMEDIATE**

Sizes

Holder: Approximately 4⅜ inches W x 3¼ inches H x 2⅜ inches D (11.1cm x 8.3cm x 6cm)

Butterfly: Approximately 3 inches W x 1⅞ inches H (7.6cm x 4.8cm)

Materials

- 2 sheets clear 10-count plastic canvas
- Small amount black 10-count plastic canvas
- Anchor #5 pearl cotton as listed in color key
- Anchor 6-strand embroidery floss as listed in color key
- #22 tapestry needle
- 2 artificial black flower stamens
- 2 (13-inch/33cm) lengths 20-gauge white stem wire
- Pencil
- Tacky craft glue or hot-glue gun

Project Note

The heart and star symbols on the butterfly graph designate Continental Stitches.

Picket Fence Holder

Cutting & Stitching

1. Cut four sides, four ends, eight posts and eight pickets from clear plastic canvas according to graphs, cutting out four holes in sides and two holes in ends.

Cut one 43-hole x 23-hole piece from clear plastic canvas for base. Two sides, two ends and base will remain unstitched.

2. Using 2 strands pearl cotton throughout, stitch eight pickets and eight posts following graphs. Stitch two sides and two ends with light charcoal gray where indicated, leaving all other areas unstitched.

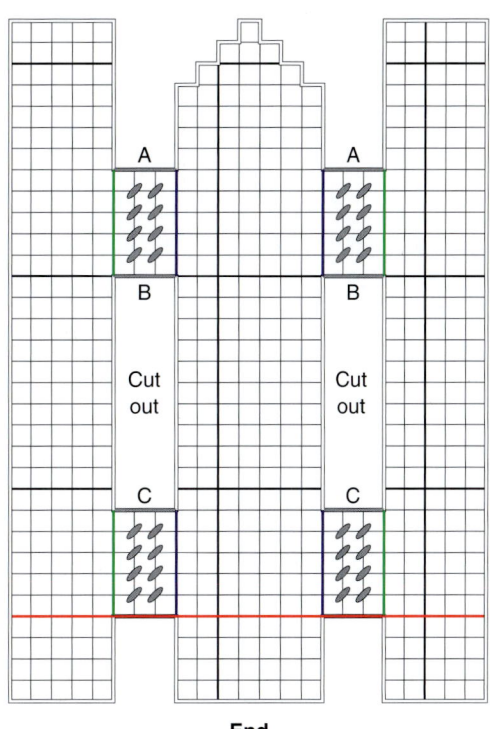

End
23 holes x 32 holes
Cut 4 from clear
Stitch 2

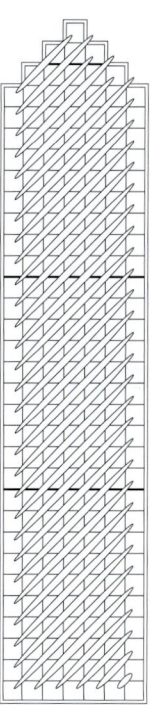

Picket
7 holes x 32 holes
Cut 8 from clear

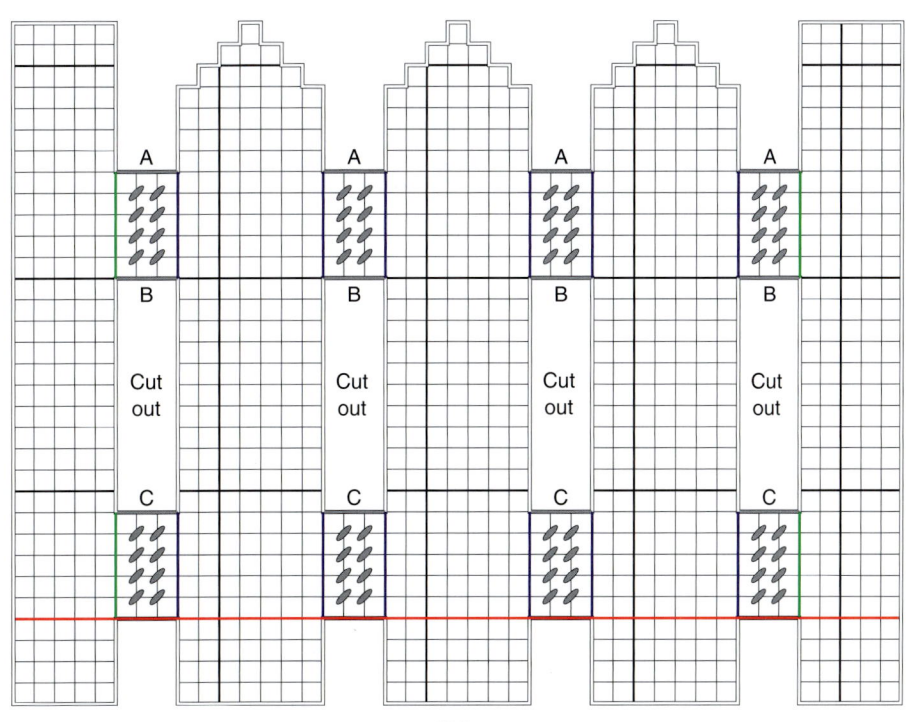

Side
43 holes x 32 holes
Cut 4 from clear
Stitch 2

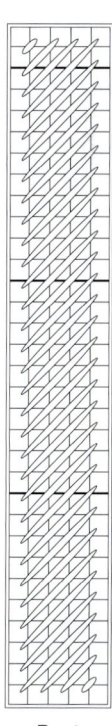

Post
5 holes x 32 holes
Cut 8 from clear

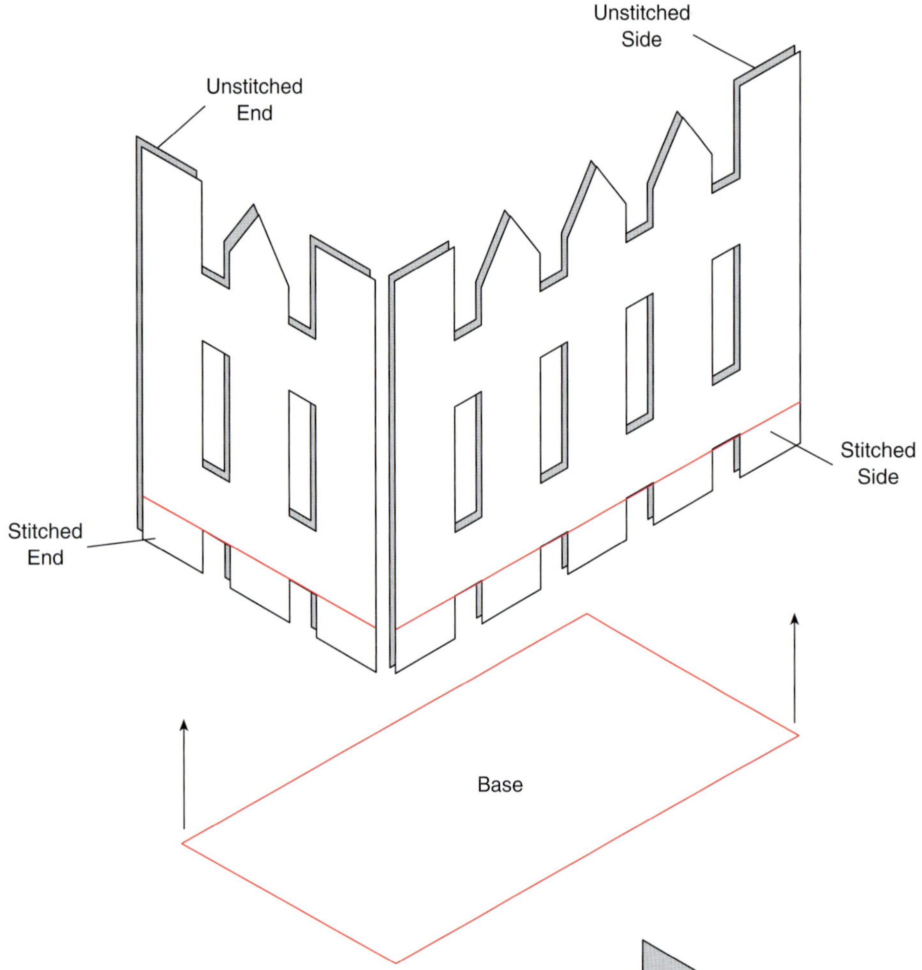

Unstitched
Side

Unstitched
End

Unstitched
Side

Stitched
Side

Stitched
End

Base

Assembly Diagram 1
Only 1 side and 1 end shown

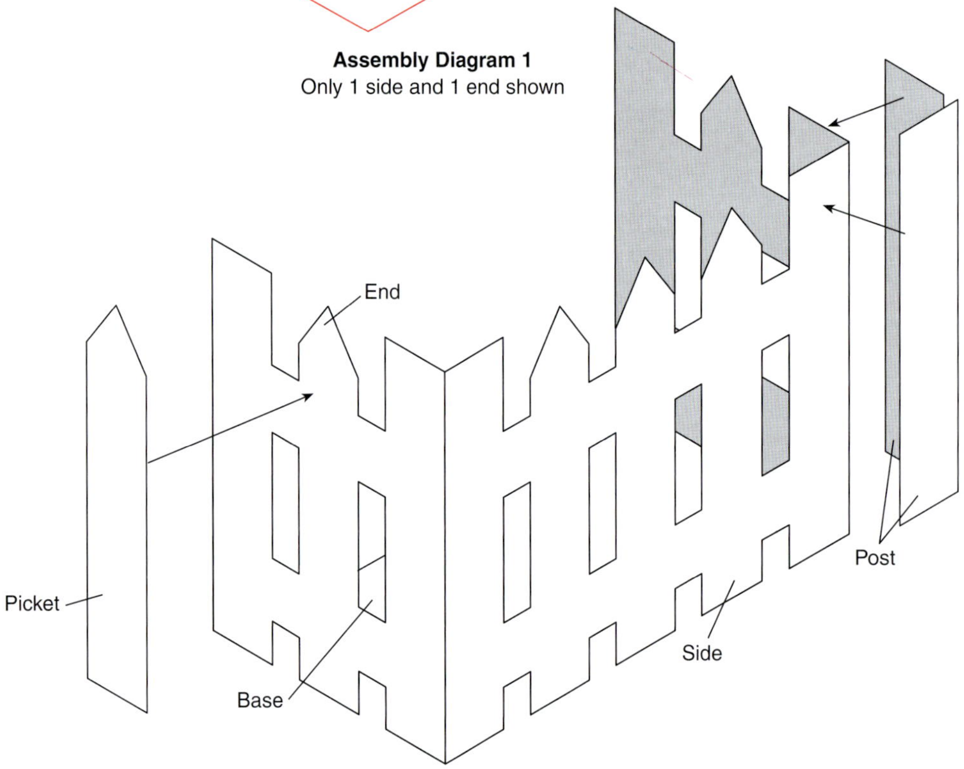

End

Picket

Base

Side

Post

Assembly Diagram 2
Only portion of holder shown

Assembly

1. Place one unstitched side behind one stitched side. Following graphs and assembly diagram 1, and using 2 strands light charcoal gray through step 3, Whipstitch edges together at A, B and C.

2. Repeat with remaining side pieces and end pieces.

3. Whipstitch unstitched base to sides and ends where indicated with red lines, working through all three layers.

4. Following graphs and assembly diagram 2, and using 2 strands white through step 5, place one stitched picket in front of each picket on fence pieces. Whipstitch together along edges (including top and bottom edges) and where indicated with blue lines on sides and ends, working through all three layers.

5. Whipstitch side edges of two posts to each corner, working through all six layers. Whipstitch remaining edges to fence edges (including top and bottom edges) and to green lines on sides and ends, working through all layers.

Butterfly

1. Cut one butterfly from clear plastic canvas and one from black plastic canvas according to graph. Black plastic canvas butterfly will remain unstitched.

2. Using 2 strands pearl cotton, stitch clear butterfly following graph, working uncoded areas with dark tangerine Continental Stitches.

3. When background stitching is completed, work Backstitches with 3 strands black floss.

4. Place unstitched butterfly behind stitched butterfly. Whipstitch together with 2 strands black pearl cotton.

5. For antennae, glue stamens to unstitched butterfly at head area. Wrap wire around pencil to curl. Insert one end of wire into bottom of butterfly; glue in place. Insert remaining end into holder base at one corner; glue in place. ●

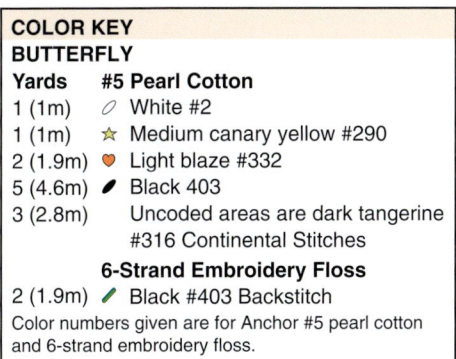

COLOR KEY

BUTTERFLY

Yards	#5 Pearl Cotton
1 (1m)	⊘ White #2
1 (1m)	★ Medium canary yellow #290
2 (1.9m)	♥ Light blaze #332
5 (4.6m)	✦ Black 403
3 (2.8m)	Uncoded areas are dark tangerine #316 Continental Stitches

6-Strand Embroidery Floss

2 (1.9m)	✦ Black #403 Backstitch

Color numbers given are for Anchor #5 pearl cotton and 6-strand embroidery floss.

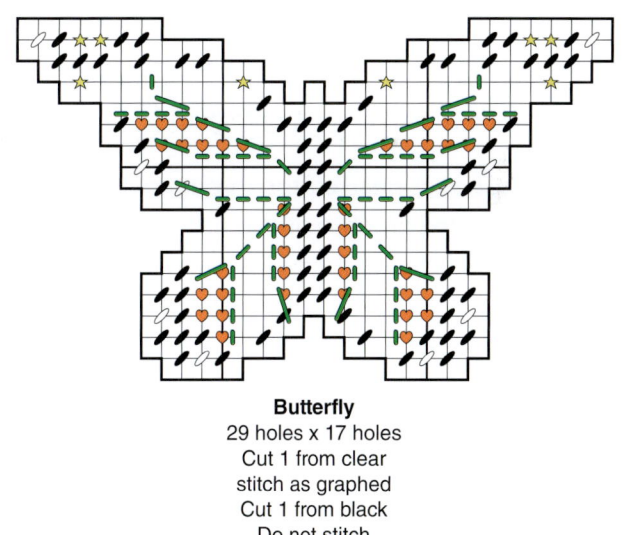

Butterfly
29 holes x 17 holes
Cut 1 from clear
stitch as graphed
Cut 1 from black
Do not stitch

Tulip

Skill Level

 INTERMEDIATE

Size

Approximately 4 inches square (10.2cm)

Materials

- ¼ sheet 10-count plastic canvas
- Anchor #5 pearl cotton as listed in color key
- Anchor 6-strand embroidery floss as listed in color key
- #22 tapestry needle
- 3⅞-inch/9.8cm square green self-adhesive felt

Project Note

The circle, heart and square symbols designate Continental Stitches.

Cutting & Stitching

1. Cut plastic canvas according to graph.

2. Using 2 strands pearl cotton throughout, stitch coaster following graph, working uncoded areas with Continental Stitches as follows: white background with medium light salmon, green background with medium emerald. Overcast with medium emerald.

3. When background stitching is completed, work Backstitches with 3 strands very dark burgundy floss.

4. Trim corners off felt to fit coaster; adhere to back side. ●

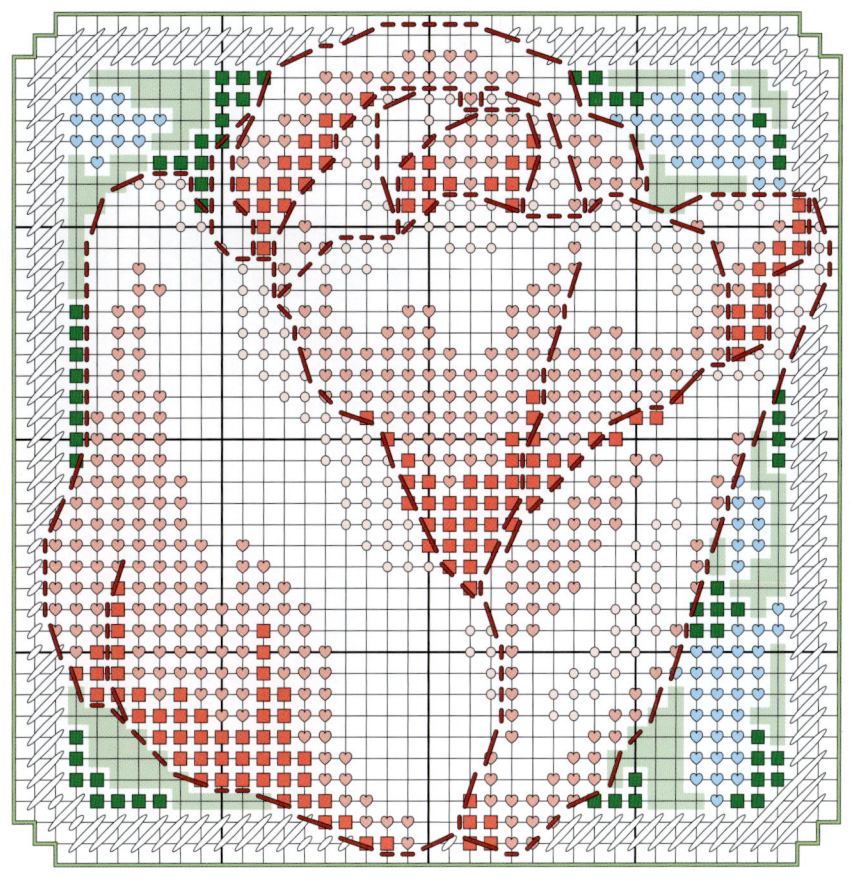

Tulip
40 holes x 40 holes
Cut 1

COLOR KEY	
TULIP	
Yards	**#5 Pearl Cotton**
7 (6.5m)	⬭ White #2
6 (5.5m)	○ Very light salmon #6
11 (10.1m)	♡ Medium dark salmon #11
5 (4.6m)	🟥 Dark salmon #13
4 (3.7m)	💙 Light emerald #225
3 (2.8m)	🟩 Very dark emerald #923
12 (11m)	Uncoded areas on white background are medium light salmon #9 Continental Stitches
7 (6.5m)	Uncoded areas on green background are medium emerald #227 Continental Stitches
	╱ Medium emerald #227 Overcast
	6-Strand Embroidery Floss
4 (3.7m)	╱ Very dark burgundy #22 Backstitch
Color numbers given are for Anchor #5 pearl cotton and 6-strand embroidery floss.	

Rose of Sharon

Skill Level
 INTERMEDIATE

Size
Approximately 4 inches square (10.2cm)

Materials
- ¼ sheet 10-count plastic canvas
- Anchor #5 pearl cotton as listed in color key
- Anchor 6-strand embroidery floss as listed in color key
- #22 tapestry needle
- 3⅞-inch/9.8cm square green self-adhesive felt

Project Note
The circle, heart and square symbols designate Continental Stitches.

Cutting & Stitching
1. Cut plastic canvas according to graph.

2. Using 2 strands pearl cotton throughout, stitch coaster following graph, working uncoded areas with Continental Stitches as follows: white background with medium light carnation, green background with medium emerald.

3. When background stitching is completed, work Backstitches with 3 strands dark carmine rose floss.

4. Trim corners off felt to fit coaster; adhere to back side. ●

Rose of Sharon
40 holes x 40 holes
Cut 1

COLOR KEY	
ROSE OF SHARON	
Yards	**#5 Pearl Cotton**
8 (7.4m)	⊘ White #2
8 (7.4m)	○ Very light carnation #24
5 (4.6m)	♥ Medium dark carnation #28
2 (1.9m)	■ Dark carmine rose #44
3 (2.8m)	♡ Light emerald #225
6 (5.5m)	■ Very dark emerald #923
12 (11m)	Uncoded areas on white background are medium light carnation #26 Continental Stitches
8 (7.4m)	Uncoded areas on green background are medium emerald #227 Continental Stitches
	╱ Medium emerald #227 Overcast
	6-Strand Embroidery Floss
4 (3.7m)	╱ Dark carmine rose #44 Backstitch

Color numbers given are for Anchor #5 pearl cotton and 6-strand embroidery floss.

Petunia

Skill Level

◼◼◼◻ INTERMEDIATE

Size

Approximately 4 inches square (10.2cm)

Materials

- ¼ sheet 10-count plastic canvas
- Anchor #5 pearl cotton as listed in color key
- Anchor 6-strand embroidery floss as listed in color key
- #22 tapestry needle
- 3⅞-inch/9.8cm square green self-adhesive felt

Project Note

The diamond, heart, inverted triangle and square symbols designate Continental Stitches.

Cutting & Stitching

1. Cut plastic canvas according to graph.

2. Using 2 strands pearl cotton throughout, stitch coaster following graph, working uncoded areas with Continental Stitches as follows: white background with white, pink background with very light salmon, green background with medium emerald. Overcast with medium emerald.

3. When background stitching is completed, work Backstitches with 3 strands dark raspberry and medium gray floss.

4. Trim corners off felt to fit coaster; adhere to back side. ●

Petunia
40 holes x 40 holes
Cut 1

COLOR KEY		
PETUNIA		
Yards		**#5 Pearl Cotton**
12 (11m)	⬭	White #2
11 (10.1m)	♥	Medium orchid #87
5 (4.6m)	⬛	Dark orchid #89
3 (2.8m)	🩵	Light emerald #225
2 (1.9m)	♦	Medium charcoal gray #235
5 (4.6m)	▽	Light gray #397
2 (1.9m)	⬭	Gray #398
4 (3.7m)	⬛	Very dark emerald #923
		Uncoded areas on white background are white #2 Continental Stitches
7 (6.5m)		Uncoded areas on pink background are very light salmon #6 Continental Stitches
8 (7.4m)		Uncoded areas on green background are medium emerald #227 Continental Stitches
	╱	Medium emerald #227 Overcast
		6-Strand Embroidery Floss
2 (1.9m)	╱	Dark raspberry #70 Backstitch
3 (2.8m)	╱	Medium gray #400 Backstitch
Color numbers given are for Anchor #5 pearl cotton and 6-strand embroidery floss.		

Poppy

Skill Level

 INTERMEDIATE

Size

Approximately 4 inches square (10.2cm)

Materials

- ¼ sheet 10-count plastic canvas
- Anchor #5 pearl cotton as listed in color key
- Anchor 6-strand embroidery floss as listed in color key
- #22 tapestry needle
- 3⅞-inch/9.8cm square green self-adhesive felt

Project Note

The diamond, heart and square symbols designate Continental Stitches.

Cutting & Stitching

1. Cut plastic canvas according to graph.

2. Using 2 strands pearl cotton throughout, stitch coaster following graph, working uncoded areas with Continental Stitches as follows: pink background with crimson red, white background with light blaze, green background with medium emerald. Overcast with medium emerald.

3. When background stitching is completed, work Backstitches with 3 strands black floss.

4. Trim corners off felt to fit coaster; adhere to back side. ●

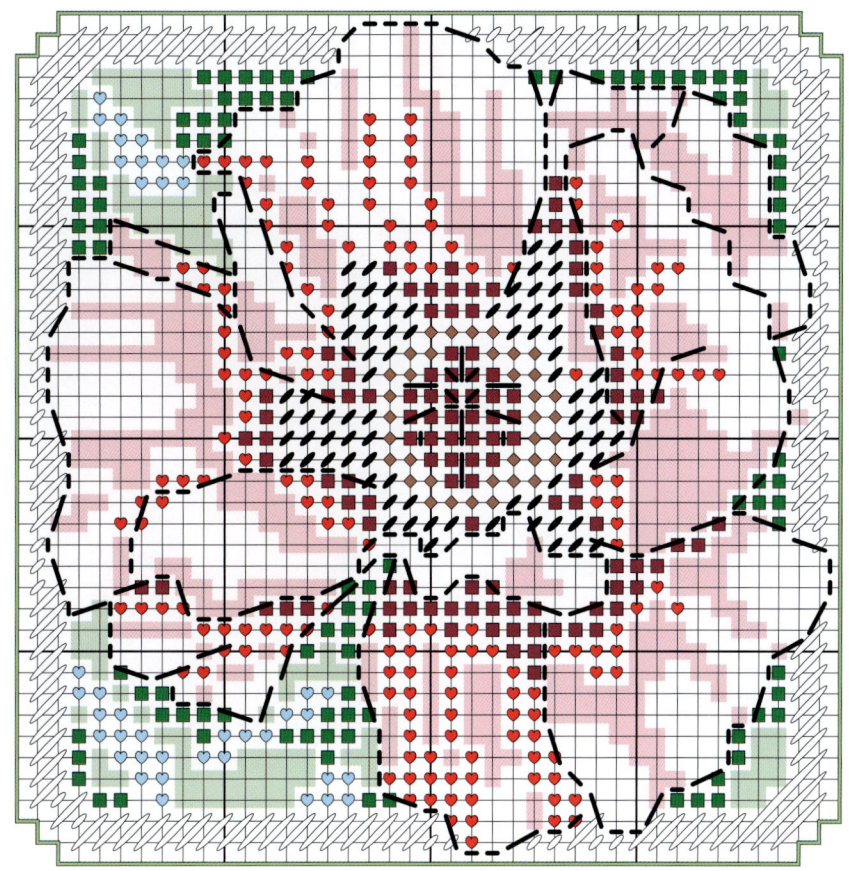

Poppy
40 holes x 40 holes
Cut 1

COLOR KEY	
POPPY	
Yards	**#5 Pearl Cotton**
6 (5.5m)	⊘ White #2
5 (4.6m)	■ Medium dark burgundy #20
6 (5.5m)	♥ Carmine red #47
3 (2.8m)	♡ Light emerald #225
2 (1.9m)	◆ Dark terra-cotta #341
3 (2.8m)	╱ Black #403
4 (3.7m)	■ Very dark emerald #923
11 (10.1m)	Uncoded areas on pink background are crimson red #46 Continental Stitches
9 (8.3m)	Uncoded areas with white background are light blaze #332 Continental Stitches
7 (6.5m)	Uncoded areas with green background are medium emerald #227 Continental Stitches
	╱ Medium emerald #227 Overcast
	6-Strand Embroidery Floss
4 (3.7m)	╱ Black #403 Backstitch
Color numbers given are for Anchor #5 pearl cotton and 6-strand embroidery floss.	

Rose

Skill Level

 INTERMEDIATE

Size

Approximately 4 inches square (10.2cm)

Materials

- ¼ sheet 10-count plastic canvas
- Anchor #5 pearl cotton as listed in color key
- Anchor 6-strand embroidery floss as listed in color key
- #22 tapestry needle
- 3⅞-inch/9.8cm square green self-adhesive felt

Project Note

The circle, heart and square symbols designate Continental Stitches.

Cutting & Stitching

1. Cut plastic canvas according to graph.

2. Using 2 strands pearl cotton throughout, stitch coaster following graph, working uncoded areas with Continental Stitches as follows: white background with medium raspberry, green background with medium emerald. Overcast with medium emerald.

3. When background stitching is completed, work Backstitches with 3 strands black floss.

4. Trim corners off felt to fit coaster; adhere to back side. ●

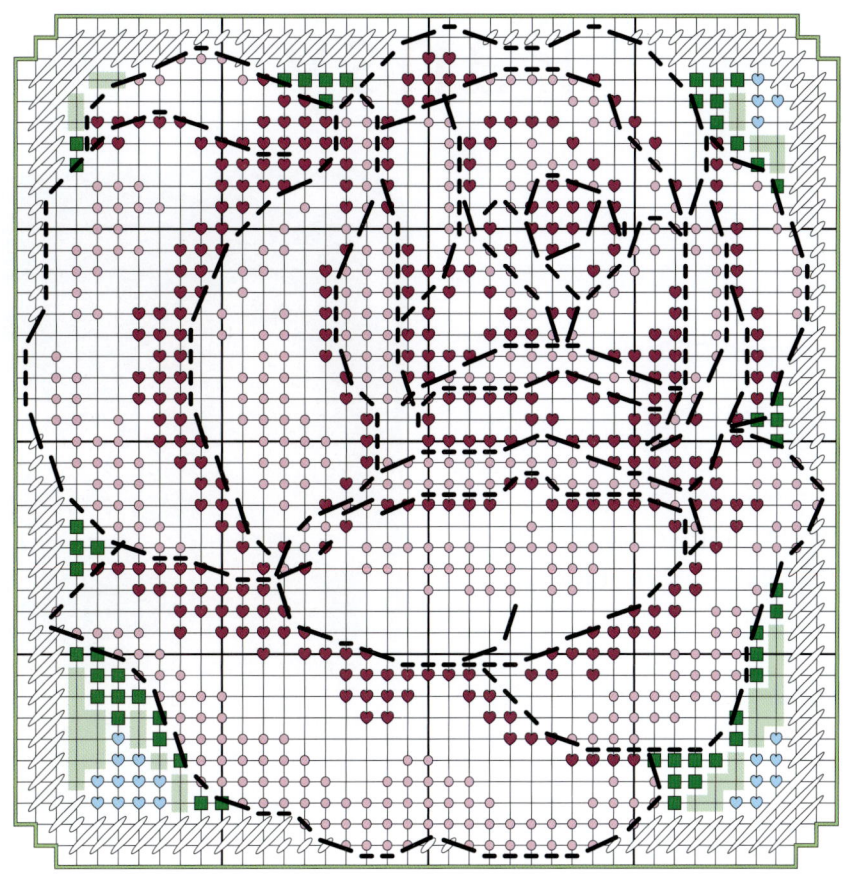

Rose
40 holes x 40 holes
Cut 1

COLOR KEY	
ROSE	
Yards	**#5 Pearl Cotton**
6 (5.5m)	⬭ White #2
11 (10.1m)	⬤ Medium light raspberry #68
12 (11m)	♥ Dark raspberry #70
2 (1.9m)	♡ Light emerald #225
3 (2.8m)	⬛ Very dark emerald #923
15 (13.8m)	Uncoded areas on white background are medium raspberry #69 Continental Stitches
6 (5.5m)	Uncoded areas on green background are medium emerald #227 Continental Stitches
	╱ Medium emerald #227 Overcast
	6-Strand Embroidery Floss
4 (3.7m)	╱ Black #403 Backstitch
Color numbers given are for Anchor #5 pearl cotton and 6-strand embroidery floss.	

Pansy

Skill Level

◼◼◼◻ INTERMEDIATE

Size

Approximately 4 inches square (10.2cm)

Materials

- ¼ sheet 10-count plastic canvas
- Anchor #5 pearl cotton as listed in color key
- Anchor 6-strand embroidery floss as listed in color key
- #22 tapestry needle
- 3⅞-inch/9.8cm square green self-adhesive felt

Project Note

The diamond, heart, inverted triangle, square and star symbols designate Continental Stitches.

Cutting & Stitching

1. Cut plastic canvas according to graph.

2. Using 2 strands pearl cotton throughout, stitch coaster following graph, working uncoded areas with Continental Stitches as follows: pink background with medium dark burgundy, lavender background with medium dark lavender, green background with medium emerald, white background with medium canary yellow. Overcast with medium emerald.

3. When background stitching is completed, work Backstitches with 3 strands black floss.

4. Trim corners off felt to fit coaster; adhere to back side. ●

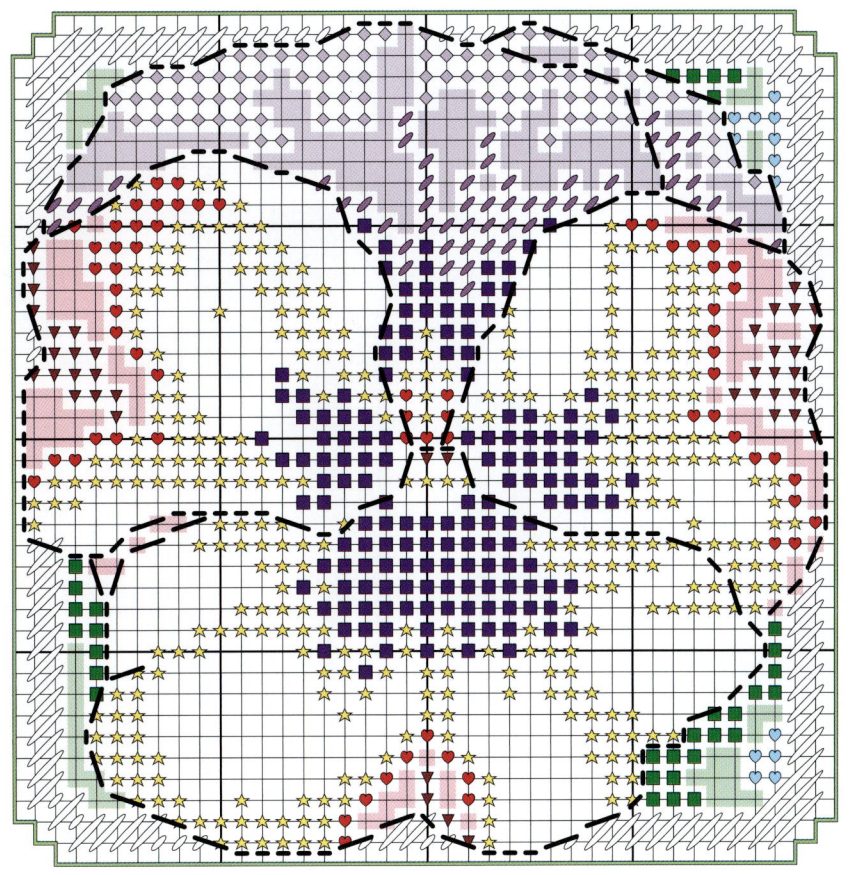

Pansy
40 holes x 40 holes
Cut 1

COLOR KEY		
PANSY		
Yards	**#5 Pearl Cotton**	
5 (4.6m)	⬭	White #2
3 (2.8m)	♥	Medium burgundy #19
3 (2.8m)	▼	Very dark burgundy #22
5 (4.6m)	■	Dark violet #101
4 (3.7m)	◆	Medium lavender #110
3 (2.8m)	⬭	Dark lavender #112
2 (1.9m)	♡	Light emerald #225
9 (8.3m)	★	Medium light topaz #306
2 (1.9m)	■	Very dark emerald #923
3 (2.8m)		Uncoded areas on pink background are medium dark burgundy #20 Continental Stitches
4 (3.7m)		Uncoded areas on lavender background are medium dark lavender #111 Continental Stitches
5 (4.6m)		Uncoded areas on green background are medium emerald #227 Continental Stitches
11 (10.1m)		Uncoded areas on white background are medium canary yellow #290 Continental Stitches
	⁄	Medium emerald #227 Overcast
	6-Strand Embroidery Floss	
4 (3.7m)	⁄	Black #403 Backstitch
Color numbers given are for Anchor #5 pearl cotton and 6-strand embroidery floss.		

Lily

Skill Level

 INTERMEDIATE

Size

Approximately 4 inches square (10.2cm)

Materials

- ¼ sheet 10-count plastic canvas
- Anchor #5 pearl cotton as listed in color key
- Anchor 6-strand embroidery floss as listed in color key
- #22 tapestry needle
- 3⅞-inch/9.8cm square green self-adhesive felt

Project Note

The diamond, heart, inverted triangle, square and star symbols designate Continental Stitches.

Cutting & Stitching

1. Cut plastic canvas according to graph.

2. Using 2 strands pearl cotton throughout, stitch coaster following graph, working uncoded areas with Continental Stitches as follows: white background with white, green background with medium emerald. Overcast with medium emerald.

3. When background stitching is completed, work Backstitches with 3 strands medium parrot green and medium gray floss.

4. Trim corners off felt to fit coaster; adhere to back side. ●

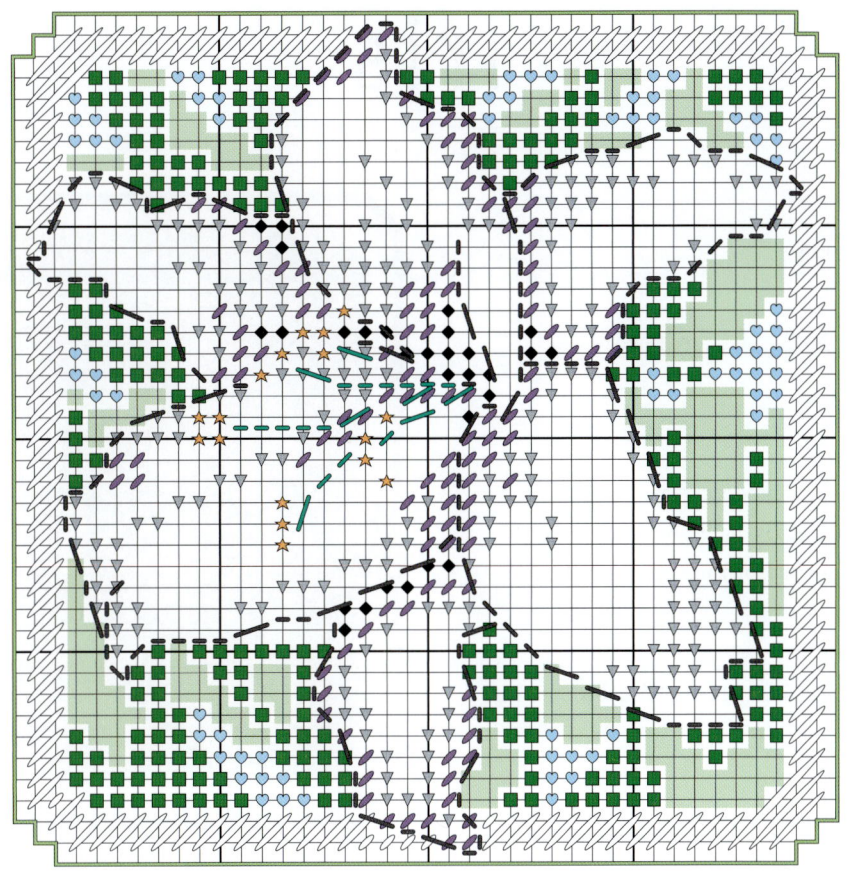

Lily
40 holes x 40 holes
Cut 1

COLOR KEY		
LILY		
Yards		**#5 Pearl Cotton**
18 (16.5m)	⊘	White #2
3 (2.8m)	🩵	Light emerald #225
2 (1.9m)	◆	Medium charcoal gray #235
2 (1.9m)	★	Light blaze #332
7 (6.5m)	▽	Light gray #397
5 (4.6m)	⬭	Gray #398
7 (6.5m)	■	Very dark emerald #923
		Uncoded areas on white background are white #2 Continental Stitches
11 (10.1m)		Uncoded areas on green background are medium emerald #227 Continental Stitches
	╱	Medium emerald #227 Overcast
		6-Strand Embroidery Floss
2 (1.9m)	╱	Medium parrot green #256 Backstitch
4 (3.7m)	╱	Medium gray #400 Backstitch

Color numbers given are for Anchor #5 pearl cotton and 6-strand embroidery floss.

Iris

Skill Level
 **INTERMEDIATE**

Size
Approximately 4 inches square (10.2cm)

Materials
- ¼ sheet 10-count plastic canvas
- Anchor #5 pearl cotton as listed in color key
- Anchor 6-strand embroidery floss as listed in color key
- #22 tapestry needle
- 3⅞-inch/9.8cm square green self-adhesive felt

Project Note
The diamond, heart, square and star symbols designate Continental Stitches.

Cutting & Stitching

1. Cut plastic canvas according to graph.

2. Using 2 strands pearl cotton throughout, stitch coaster following graph, working uncoded areas with Continental Stitches as follows: white background with medium lavender, green background with medium emerald. Overcast with medium emerald.

3. When background stitching is completed, work Backstitches with 3 strands black floss.

4. Trim corners off felt to fit coaster; adhere to back side. ●

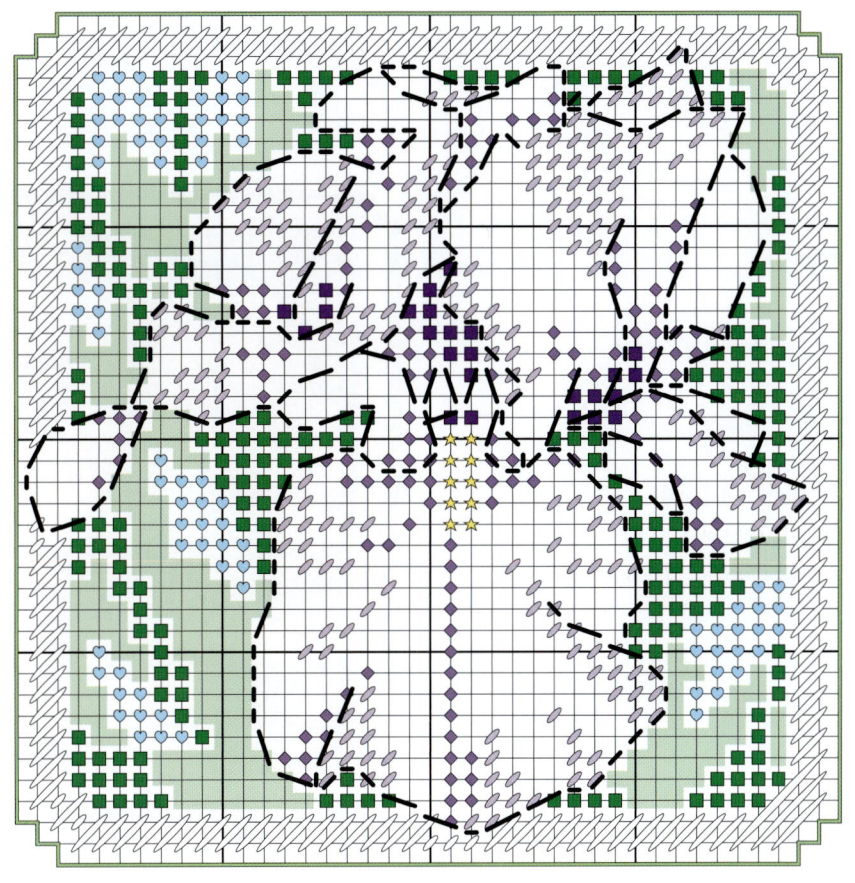

Iris
40 holes x 40 holes
Cut 1

COLOR KEY	
IRIS	
Yards	**#5 Pearl Cotton**
7 (6.5m)	⬭ White #2
2 (1.9m)	■ Dark violet #101
7 (6.5m)	⬭ Medium light lavender #109
6 (5.5m)	◆ Dark lavender #112
4 (3.7m)	♡ Light emerald #225
2 (1.9m)	☆ Light topaz #305
7 (6.5m)	■ Very dark emerald #923
12 (11m)	Uncoded areas on white background are medium lavender #110 Continental Stitches
10 (9.2m)	Uncoded areas on green background are medium emerald #227 Continental Stitches
	⬭ Medium emerald #227 Overcast
	6-Strand Embroidery Floss
4 (3.7m)	╱ Black #403 Backstitch

Color numbers given are for Anchor #5 pearl cotton and 6-strand embroidery floss.

Daffodil

Skill Level

■ ■ ■ ▭ INTERMEDIATE

Size

Approximately 4 inches square (10.2cm)

Materials

- ¼ sheet 10-count plastic canvas
- Anchor #5 pearl cotton as listed in color key
- Anchor 6-strand embroidery floss as listed in color key
- #22 tapestry needle
- 3⅞-inch/9.8cm square green self-adhesive felt

Project Note

The diamond, heart, square and star symbols designate Continental Stitches.

Cutting & Stitching

1. Cut plastic canvas according to graph.

2. Using 2 strands pearl cotton throughout, stitch coaster following graph, working uncoded areas with Continental Stitches as follows: white background with medium canary yellow, green background with medium emerald. Overcast with medium emerald.

3. When background stitching is completed, work Backstitches with 3 strands very dark topaz floss.

4. Trim corners off felt to fit coaster; adhere to back side. ●

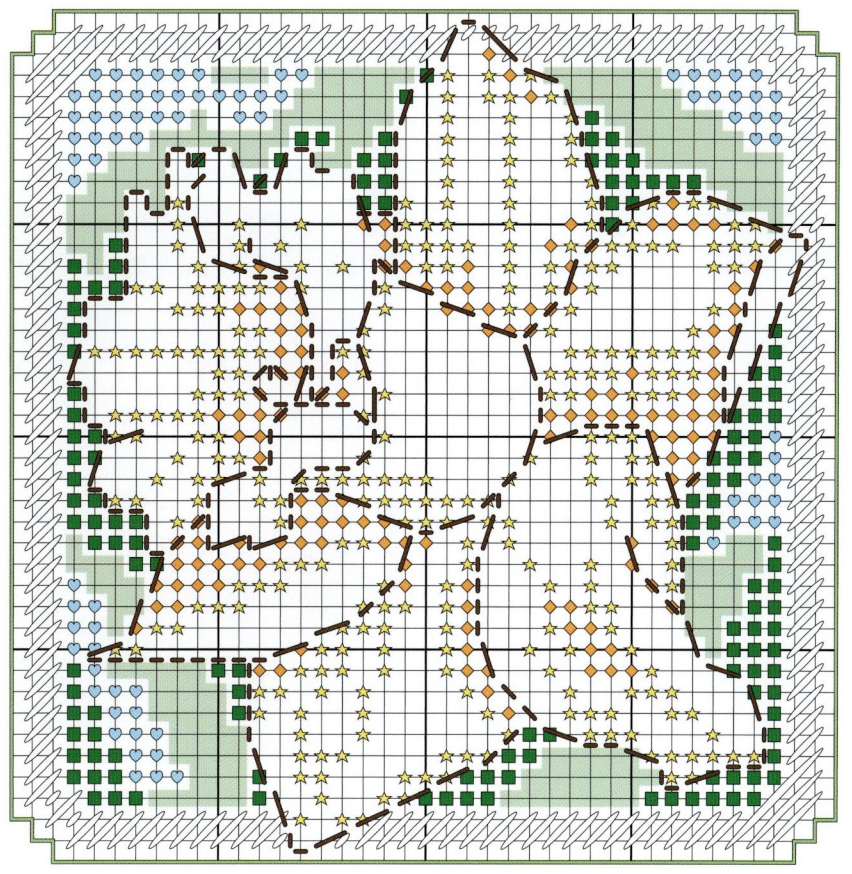

Daffodil
40 holes x 40 holes
Cut 1

COLOR KEY		
DAFFODIL		
Yards		**#5 Pearl Cotton**
7 (6.5m)	⬭	White #2
4 (3.7m)	💙	Light emerald #225
10 (9.2m)	⭐	Medium light topaz #306
5 (4.6m)	🔶	Medium dark topaz #308
6 (5.5m)	◼	Very dark emerald #923
14 (12.9m)		Uncoded areas on white background are medium canary yellow #290 Continental Stitches
6 (5.5m)		Uncoded areas on green background are medium emerald #227 Continental Stitches
	╱	Medium emerald #227 Overcast
6-Strand Embroidery Floss		
4 (3.7m)	╱	Very dark topaz #310 Backstitch

Color numbers given are for Anchor #5 pearl cotton and 6-strand embroidery floss.

Columbine

Skill Level

 INTERMEDIATE

Size

Approximately 4 inches square (10.2cm)

Materials

- ¼ sheet 10-count plastic canvas
- Anchor #5 pearl cotton as listed in color key
- Anchor 6-strand embroidery floss as listed in color key
- #22 tapestry needle
- 3⅞-inch/9.8cm square green self-adhesive felt

Project Note

The heart, square and star symbols designate Continental Stitches.

Cutting & Stitching

1. Cut plastic canvas according to graph.

2. Using 2 strands pearl cotton throughout, stitch coaster following graph, working uncoded areas with Continental Stitches as follows: white background with medium dark burgundy, green background with medium emerald. Overcast with medium emerald.

3. When background stitching is completed work Backstitches with 3 strands very dark topaz and black floss.

4. Trim corners off felt to fit coaster; adhere to back side. ●

Columbine
40 holes x 40 holes
Cut 1

COLOR KEY		
COLUMBINE		
Yards		**#5 Pearl Cotton**
7 (6.5m)	⬭	White #2
4 (3.7m)	🟣	Medium burgundy #19
6 (5.5m)	🟥	Very dark burgundy #22
5 (4.6m)	💙	Light emerald #225
4 (3.7m)	⬭	Medium canary yellow #290
3 (2.8m)	★	Medium light topaz #306
9 (8.3m)	🟩	Very dark emerald #923
5 (4.6m)		Uncoded areas on white background are medium dark burgundy #20 Continental Stitches
13 (11.9m)		Uncoded areas on green background are medium emerald #227 Continental Stitches
	✦	Medium emerald #227 Overcast
6-Strand Embroidery Floss		
2 (1.9m)	✦	Very dark topaz #310 Backstitch
5 (4.6m)	✦	Black #403 Backstitch
Color numbers given are for Anchor #5 pearl cotton and 6-strand embroidery floss.		

Clematis

Skill Level
 INTERMEDIATE

Size
Approximately 4 inches square (10.2cm)

Materials
- ¼ sheet 10-count plastic canvas
- Anchor #5 pearl cotton as listed in color key
- Anchor 6-strand embroidery floss as listed in color key
- #22 tapestry needle
- 3⅞-inch/9.8cm square green self-adhesive felt

Project Note
The circle, diamond, heart, square and star symbols designate Continental Stitches.

Cutting & Stitching
1. Cut plastic canvas according to graph.

2. Using 2 strands pearl cotton throughout, stitch coaster following graph, working uncoded areas with Continental Stitches as follows: white background with medium light lavender, green background with medium emerald. Overcast with medium emerald.

3. When background stitching is completed, work Backstitches with 3 strands very dark violet floss.

4. Trim corners off felt to fit coaster; adhere to back side. ●

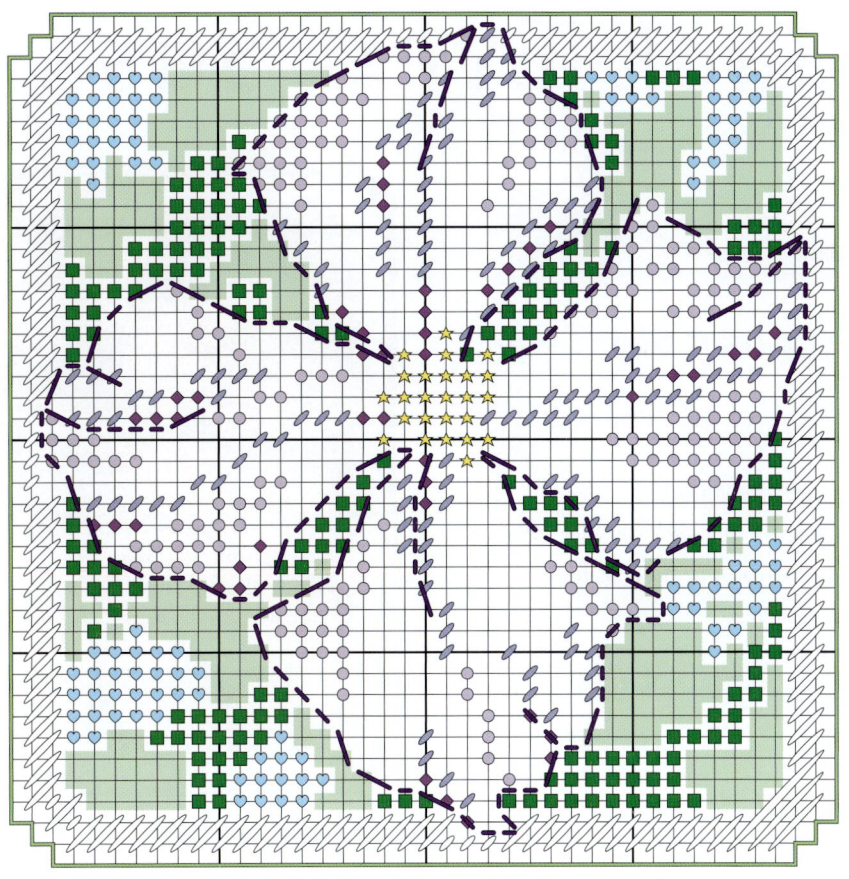

Clematis
40 holes x 40 holes
Cut 1

COLOR KEY		
CLEMATIS		
Yards		**#5 Pearl Cotton**
7 (6.5m)	⬭	White #2
6 (5.5m)	⬤	Light lavender #108
5 (4.6m)	⬭	Medium lavender #110
3 (2.8m)	◆	Dark lavender #112
4 (3.7m)	♡	Light emerald #225
2 (1.9m)	☆	Light topaz #305
6 (5.5m)	■	Very dark emerald #923
12 (11m)		Uncoded areas on white background are medium light lavender #109 Continental Stitches
11 (10.1m)		Uncoded areas on green background are medium emerald #227 Continental Stitches
	⁄	Medium emerald #227 Overcast
6-Strand Embroidery Floss		
4 (3.7m)	⁄	Very dark violet #102 Backstitch
Color numbers given are for Anchor #5 pearl cotton and 6-strand embroidery floss.		

Black-Eyed Susan

Skill Level

 **INTERMEDIATE**

Size

Approximately 4 inches square (10.2cm)

Materials

- ¼ sheet 10-count plastic canvas
- Anchor #5 pearl cotton as listed in color key
- Anchor 6-strand embroidery floss as listed in color key
- #22 tapestry needle
- 3⅞-inch/9.8cm square green self-adhesive felt

Project Note

The heart, square, star and triangle symbols designate Continental Stitches.

Cutting & Stitching

1. Cut plastic canvas according to graph.

2. Using 2 strands pearl cotton throughout, stitch coaster following graph, working uncoded areas with Continental Stitches as follows: white background with medium canary yellow, green background with medium emerald. Overcast with medium emerald.

3. When background stitching is completed, work Backstitches with 3 strands very dark topaz floss.

4. Trim corners off felt to fit coaster; adhere to back side. ●

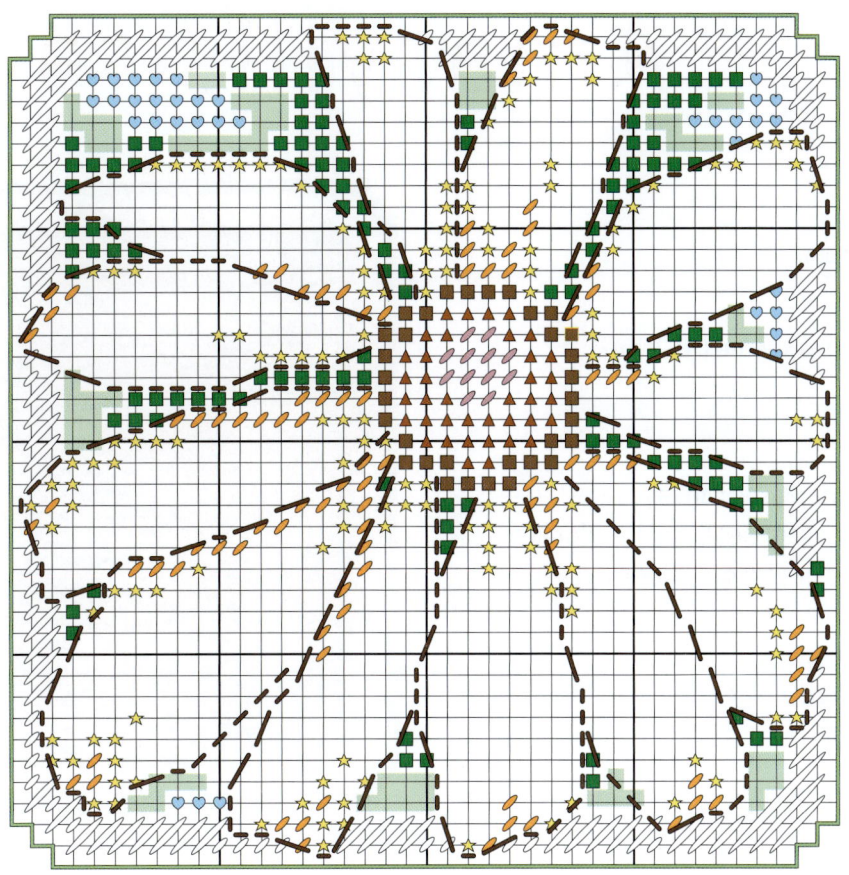

Black-Eyed Susan
40 holes x 40 holes
Cut 1

COLOR KEY	
BLACK-EYED SUSAN	
Yards	**#5 Pearl Cotton**
7 (6.5m)	⬭ White #2
3 (2.8m)	🩵 Light emerald #225
6 (5.5m)	⭐ Medium light topaz #306
4 (3.7m)	⬭ Medium dark topaz #308
2 (1.9m)	■ Dark coffee #360
2 (1.9m)	▲ Dark spice #371
2 (1.9m)	⬭ Medium rose wine #895
5 (4.6m)	■ Very dark emerald #923
23 (21.1m)	Uncoded areas on white background are medium canary yellow #290 Continental Stitches
6 (5.5m)	Uncoded areas on green background are medium emerald #227 Continental Stitches
	╱ Medium emerald #227 Overcast
6-Strand Embroidery Floss	
4 (3.7m)	╱ Very dark topaz #310 Backstitch
Color numbers given are for Anchor #5 pearl cotton and 6-strand embroidery floss.	

Amaryllis

Skill Level

 INTERMEDIATE

Size

Approximately 4 inches square (10.2cm)

Materials

- ¼ sheet 10-count plastic canvas
- Anchor #5 pearl cotton as listed in color key
- Anchor 6-strand embroidery floss as listed in color key
- #22 tapestry needle
- 3⅞-inch/9.8cm square green self-adhesive felt

Project Note

The heart, square and star symbols designate Continental Stitches.

Cutting & Stitching

1. Cut plastic canvas according to graph.

2. Using 2 strands pearl cotton throughout, stitch coaster following graph, working uncoded areas with Continental Stitches as follows: white background with carmine red, green background with medium emerald. Overcast with medium emerald.

3. When background stitching is completed, work Backstitches and Straight Stitches with 3 strands dark blaze and black floss.

4. Trim corners off felt to fit coaster; adhere to back side. ●

Amaryllis
40 holes x 40 holes
Cut 1

COLOR KEY		
AMARYLLIS		
Yards	**#5 Pearl Cotton**	
7 (6.5m)	⬭	White #2
4 (3.7m)	●	Medium dark burgundy #20
2 (1.9m)	■	Very dark burgundy #22
12 (11m)	╱	Crimson red #46
3 (2.8m)	♥	Light emerald #225
2 (1.9m)	★	Medium light topaz #306
5 (4.6m)	■	Very dark emerald #923
13 (11.9m)		Uncoded areas on white background are carmine red #47 Continental Stitches
10 (9.2m)		Uncoded areas on green background are medium emerald #227 Continental Stitches
	╱	Medium emerald #227 Overcast
6-Strand Embroidery Floss		
1 (1m)	╱	Dark blaze #335 Backstitch and Straight Stitch
4 (3.7m)	╱	Black #403 Backstitch
Color numbers given are for Anchor #5 pearl cotton and 6-strand embroidery floss.		

Getting Started

Before You Cut

Buy one brand of canvas for each entire project as brands can differ slightly in the distance between bars. Count holes carefully from the graph before you cut, using the bolder lines that show every 10 holes. These 10-count lines begin from the left side for vertical lines and from the bottom for horizontal lines. Mark canvas before cutting; then remove all marks completely before stitching. If the piece is cut in a rectangular or square shape and is either not worked, or worked with only one color and one type of stitch, the graph may not be included in the pattern. Instead, the cutting and stitching instructions are given in the general instructions or with the individual project instructions.

Covering the Canvas

Bring needle up from back of work, leaving a short length of yarn on back of canvas; work over short length to secure. To end a thread, weave needle and thread through the wrong side of your last few stitches; clip. Follow the numbers on the small graphs beside each stitch illustration; bring your needle up from the back of the work on odd numbers and down through the front of the work on even numbers. Work embroidery stitches last, after the canvas has been completely covered by the needlepoint stitches.

Shopping for Supplies

For supplies, first shop your local craft and needlework stores. Some supplies may be found in fabric, hardware and discount stores. If you are unable to find the supplies you need, please visit AnniesCraftStore.com.

METRIC KEY:
millimeters = (mm) meters = (m)
centimeters = (cm) grams = (g)

Basic Stitches

Continental

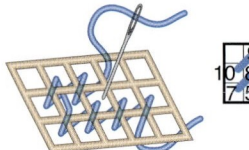

Cross

Long

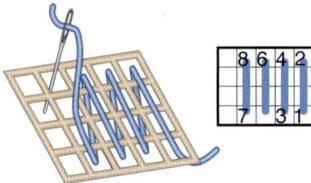

Slanted Gobelin

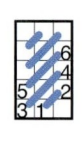

Whipstitch

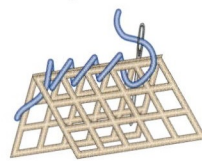

Overcast

Embroidery Stitches

Backstitch

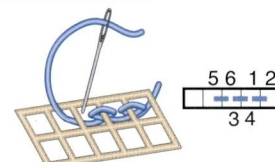

Lazy Daisy

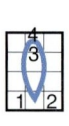

Straight

French Knot

Annie's®

Plastic Canvas Flower Coasters is published by Annie's, 306 East Parr Road, Berne, IN 46711. Printed in USA. Copyright © 2016, 2017 Annie's. All rights reserved. This publication may not be reproduced in part or in whole without written permission from the publisher.

RETAIL STORES: If you would like to carry this publication or any other Annie's publication, visit AnniesWSL.com.

Every effort has been made to ensure that the instructions in this publication are complete and accurate. We cannot, however, take responsibility for human error, typographical mistakes or variations in individual work. Please visit AnniesCustomerService.com to check for pattern updates.

ISBN: 978-1-59012-635-6

2 3 4 5 6 7 8 9